Ferrets

Ferrets

Mary Berendes

THE CHILD'S WORLD®, INC.

Library of Congress Cataloging-in-Publication Data
Berendes, Mary.
Ferrets / by Mary Berendes.
p.   cm.
Includes index.
Summary: Discusses the physical characteristics,
behavior, habitat, and life cycle of ferrets.
ISBN 1-56766-477-6 (lib. reinforced : alk. paper)
1. Ferret—Juvenile literature.
[1. Ferret.]   I Title.
QL737.C25B46   1998
599.76′629—dc21   97-35223
CIP
AC

Photo Credits

© Jeff Vanuga: cover, 6, 13, 15, 24, 26
© Beth Davidow: 19, 20, 30
© Ron Kimball: 2, 9, 10, 29
ANIMALS ANIMALS © E.R. Degginger: 23
© William Muñoz: 16

On the cover...

Front cover: This *black-footed ferret* has just come out of its burrow.
Page 2: This *domestic ferret* has shiny fur.

Table of Contents

As darkness falls over the prairie, many things begin to happen. Owls hoot as the wind blows through the grass. Mice and rabbits nibble and munch on grasses and seeds. Suddenly, another small animal appears on the prairie. It sniffs the ground as it creeps quietly along. What could this creature be? It's a ferret!

This *black-footed ferret* is hunting as the sun goes down.

What Are Ferrets?

Ferrets belong to a group of animals called **mammals**. Mammals have hair all over their bodies. They have warm blood and feed their babies milk from their bodies. Cats, dogs, and people are mammals, too.

Ferrets have many animal relatives. Weasels, otters, skunks, and wolverines are all related to ferrets. All of these animals are known for their shiny, beautiful fur coats.

This *domestic ferret* is sniffing the air.

Ferrets come in all kinds of colors. Some are a creamy yellow. Others have black feet. Some ferrets are even white! All ferrets have long, skinny bodies and four short legs with sharp, curved claws. They also have long tails. Ferrets often have "masks" on their faces. This is just dark fur near their eyes.

Domestic ferrets like this one are very beautiful.

Are There Different Kinds of Ferrets?

There are two kinds of ferrets. *Domestic ferrets* are very common. They are about two feet long and can weigh up to five pounds. They are very smart and playful. In fact, many people raise domestic ferrets as pets. They care for them and love them just as they would a cat or a dog.

Black-footed ferrets are named for their black feet. The rest of their bodies are a dull yellow. They have dark masks of fur on their faces. They also have black fur on the tips of their tails.

It is easy to see how black-footed ferrets got their name.

Black-footed ferrets live in grasslands called *prairies*. These ferrets are **endangered**, which means they are in danger of dying out. Not very long ago, black-footed ferrets lived on almost every prairie in North America. They found plenty of their favorite food—a little animal called a *prairie dog*.

But as more people began to move onto the prairies, the prairie dogs had fewer places to live and eat. Many prairie dogs became sick and died. Without prairie dogs for food, many black-footed ferrets died, too.

The face of this black-footed ferret is dirty from hunting.

Today, there are almost no black-footed ferrets left in the wild. But many scientists are trying to save them. They give the ferrets warm, safe homes with plenty of food and water.

With luck, the ferrets mate and have babies. Over time, these babies grow healthy and strong. When there are enough black-footed ferrets in these safe areas, the scientists return them to the wild. Then the ferrets are left alone to find their own homes and run free.

These black-footed ferrets have been given a safe home for a while.   17

Where Do Ferrets Live?

Ferrets live in **burrows**, or tunnels, left behind by other animals. In fact, most wild ferrets live in burrows left behind by their favorite food—the prairie dog! Inside its burrow, a ferret sleeps in a **den**, or resting place. The den is also where the ferret raises its babies.

These ferrets are sleeping in their den in a Montana zoo.

Most ferrets like to live alone. They do not like other ferrets hunting or living in the same area. To avoid fighting, a ferret marks an area with smells. The ferret sprays a strong smell called *musk* on nearby trees and bushes. This smell tells other ferrets to "Stay away!"

This *albino domestic ferret* has just finished spraying its area.

What Are Baby Ferrets Like?

A male ferret is called a **hob**. A female ferret is called a **jill**. Six weeks after a hob and a jill mate, about five baby ferrets are born. The babies are called **kits**. Newborn kits cannot see or hear and are very helpless. They stay near their mother and drink her milk for about two months.

Every day, the kits grow bigger and stronger. Soon their mother teaches them how to hunt and to escape danger. When they are ready, the kits leave the den and go to live on their own.

These kits are drinking milk from their mother.

Ferrets are **carnivores**, which means they eat other animals. Rabbits, mice, squirrels, and birds are favorite foods. But the most important food for black-footed ferrets is the prairie dog.

Ferrets are mostly **nocturnal** animals. That means they are active at night and sleep during the day. At night, ferrets can find many of their favorite foods. To find a meal, a ferret sniffs around with its sensitive nose. Soon it finds an animal that would make a tasty treat. Slowly and quietly, it creeps up on its victim, called its **prey**. When it is close enough, the ferret quickly bites the animal's neck and kills it.

This black-footed ferret is beginning to hunt as the sun sets.

Many of the ferrets' prey live in underground tunnels. But the ferrets' long, skinny bodies are perfect for hunting in these tight places. Using their strong legs, the ferrets wriggle along until they find their next meal.

Ferrets like to eat their food in safe places. If a ferret kills its prey out in the open, it drags the meal into its den or an open tunnel. When it is finished eating, the ferret licks its fur until it is clean and shiny.

This black-footed ferret is coming out of a prairie dog burrow.

Do Ferrets Have Any Enemies?

Many animals like to eat ferrets. Owls, coyotes, badgers, and eagles are all ferret-hunters. But the ferret has a few tricks to scare away its enemies. If it is frightened, it hisses like a cat or barks loudly to scare its attacker away. If those tricks don't work, the ferret sprays its smelly musk and tries to get away.

This albino domestic ferret is getting ready to hiss.

Ferrets are very beautiful and smart animals. But we must learn to be more careful with nature if we want them to survive in the wild. If we care for our prairies and the animals that ferrets need to eat, then these wonderful creatures will be around for a long time to come.

This black-footed ferret has been returned to the wild.

Glossary

burrow (BUR–row)
A burrow is a tunnel that animals make underground. Ferrets live in burrows other animals leave behind.

carnivores (KAR-nih-vorz)
Carnivores are animals that eat other animals. Ferrets are carnivores.

den (DEN)
A den is a space where an animal rests and raises its babies. A ferret's den is in its burrow.

endangered (en-DANE-jerd)
When an animal is endangered, it is in danger of dying out. Black-footed ferrets are endangered.

hob (HOB)
A hob is a male ferret. Hobs live alone except when they mate.

jill (JILL)
A jill is a female ferret. Jills live alone except when they mate and raise their babies.

kits (KITS)
Baby ferrets are called kits. Kits live with their mother for several months.

mammals (MA–mullz)
Mammals are animals that have hair and warm bodies, and feed their babies milk from their bodies. Ferrets, cats, dogs, and people are all mammals.

nocturnal (nok-TUR-null)
Nocturnal animals are active at night and sleep during the day. Ferrets are mostly nocturnal.

prey (PRAY)
Prey is an animal that is hunted and eaten by another animal. Prairie dogs, mice, and rabbits are prey for ferrets.

Index